Crimson Coat

Crimson Coat

POEMS

Bruce Fessenden

GOLDENSTONE PRESS

Benson, North Carolina

Published by Goldenstone Press
P.O. Box 7
Benson, North Carolina 27504
www.goldenstonepress.com

ISBN: 978-0-9832261-5-4

Cover photo and design: Mary Jane Taylor

Book design: Eva Leong Casey and Lee Nichol

Printed in USA

GOLDENSTONE PRESS

GOLDENSTONE PRESS seeks to make original spiritual thought available as a
force of individual, cultural, and world revitalization. The press is an integral
dimension of the work of the School of Spiritual Psychology. The mission of the
School includes restoring the book as a way of inner transformation and awaken-
ing to spirit. We recognize that secondary thought and the reduction of books to
sources of information and entertainment as the dominant meaning of reading
places in jeopardy the unique character of writing as a vessel of the human spirit.
We feel that the continuing emphasis of such a narrowing of what books are
intended to be needs to be balanced by writing, editing, and publishing that em-
phasizes the act of reading as entering into a magical, even miraculous spiritual
realm that stimulates the imagination and makes possible discerning reality from
illusion in the world. The editorial board of Goldenstone Press is committed to
fostering authors with the capacity of creative spiritual imagination who write
in forms that bring readers into deep engagement with an inner transformative
process rather than being spectators to someone's speculations. A complete cata-
logue of all our books may be found at *www.goldenstonepress.com*. The web page
for the School of Spiritual Psychology is *www.spiritualschool.org*.

10 9 8 7 6 5 4 3 2 1

Dedicated to
The School of Spiritual Psychology
and Robert and Cheryl

Contents

Introduction

It is an honor to introduce this completely astounding book
of poems by Bruce Fessenden. Surely a poet, or perhaps
a literary critic rather than a psychologist concerned with
spiritual matters, should be authoring this commentary. The
only reason—an admittedly threadbare one—guiding this
introduction concerns the utterly unusual nature of these
poems. They are unusual in form, sustain an unheard-of depth
of emotion, and are an immanent form of spirituality—that is,
plunging the depths of emotion opens to the spiritual regions of
the soul.

This writing is unlike any poetry I have ever read. I do feel
an affinity between what Bruce Fesssenden writes and the
poetry of Robert Duncan, Denise Levertov, and Robert Creeley.
Bruce's poetry, though, does not have the "intellectual" ferment
carried by these poets. His poetry is direct and immediate,
speaking right from within the depths of the soul, resounding
within life. And it is intensely spiritual without announcing
itself as such. It does seem to me, though, to share the kind of
intensity that Duncan spoke of at a reading he did at the San
Francisco Museum of Art on December 11, 1963:

> What I call the Divine is what I begin to divine in
> the poem . . . The dream, the dance, the falling-in-
> love, and the poem seem to me to be of one kind. A
> seizure, given to us, overcoming the pose of the ego,
> commanding us to attend the need, enthralling us in
> the spell of a form we must achieve. To be a poet is
> to be prepared for that seizure, to have learned in the
> hand all the command one has of language, to have
> a tongue that is ready and true to the heart so that
> speech may come when the mind is not yours.[1]

---

[1] Review of "The Ambassador from Venus: Robert Duncan" by Paul
Nelson – http://bigbridge.org/BB17/reviews/Paul_Nelson.html

Even though Bruce Fessenden, as far as I know, does not have a relationship with the poetry community of the San Francisco area, and the forever lingering presence of Robert Duncan, we can nonetheless imaginally connect his poetry with the San Francisco Renaissance, and perhaps can even hear memorial resonances with Charles Olson and the Black Mountain school of poetry. These are the sorts of poetics, at any rate, that Bruce is comfortable with because they take the heart and its rhythms as central to the poetic act.

Then, there is a second relation that presents itself as of some significance. I worked extensively and intensively with James Hillman for a number of years, particularly during the time that he was intimately friendly with the poets mentioned above. James was accompanied in several conferences during the 1970s by Duncan, Levertov, and Creeley. He wanted to work with them because he saw that the deepest concerns of archetypal psychology—centering directly on the autonomy of emotion within the psyche—found strong resonance with these poets. It is this care for emotion that brings the two, Hillman and Fessenden, into relation.

Duncan's way of poetry has been called "Field Poetry." I take this term to mean that a "'feeling field" creates a poem-in-whole that goes beyond—but always takes a path through—the particularities, and dissolves the particularities into flowing, coming-to-be forms. This kind of poetics certainly holds for Bruce Fessenden. And because his poetic imagination concentrates wholly and completely on emotion-as-field, we can perhaps feel his poetry as a creative uniting of Duncan with Hillman—if we don't take such a suggestion literally. The intensely personal nature of Bruce's poetry takes up the material of his life, forming biographical matter into poetic form, dissolving the "only personal" nature, making the substance of emotion a resonance of everyone's emotional being, felt wholly.

Bruce enters into the emotional biography of life, stays with it, deepens it, continues to deepen it, never leaves this domain for a moment, never speaks for it, but allows it to reveal itself, and then, in quite unexpected moments, there are glimmers of light, true Light. It is spiritual without putting on any pretense of being "spiritual." He inherently, and rightly, distrusts, I think, throwing around the word "spiritual" in religious, metaphysical, theological, and most of all, personal ways. The word "spiritual" may well be one of our most misused words. When life itself has thrown one into the completely unknown—beyond one's own making or control—it is the resulting way of life, if one can stay with it, that reveals spiritual presences, unnamed, but deeply felt. What surprises most in these poems is that the "disturbances" are themselves the domain of action that forms, shapes, moves, anticipates, and reveals the ever-present invisible forming forces of human existence.

Bearing difficult emotions, living at the collective edge, coming close every moment to inward poverty, seeking the significance of the impossible, refusing to interpret the dire circumstances one has come from, living in faith that there is some unknown and holy reason for pain suffered—this is the realm of imagination within which these poems take place.

The emotion of these poems constellates around family, as one might anticipate. Father, mother, partners are here approached with care of the emotions, not simply enduring, or trying to find an escape from the seemingly questionable gift of a terribly troublesome family. Such tending opens emotion to the larger world where it emerges as feeling, as being in touch with feeling; and feeling as the way to be in touch with the immediacy of the natural world, and nature opening to the whole of the mystery of human existence as inseparable from the mystery of nature and world.

One never seems to get very far into the world with psychology, certainly not as far as this poetry does, for trauma psychology always approaches the emotion of family life as something gone wrong. This poetry cannot be rightly understood as coming to terms with "something gone wrong"; it is, rather, the working of fate, which, when openly embraced, every corner of it, suddenly

shows its true face as that of destiny, and destiny as Life—
Life beyond biologic life, Life beyond personal life, Life as
sometimes bumpy, but always-seeking-harmony with the whole
of existence.

Without the motion of e-motion, world remains an illusory
vision of self-interest with the wider world as only a backdrop.
The true character of the world as a theatre of incessant
action—changing perpetually, actors coming in and out, with
serious or dramatic or comic parts assigned by eternal nature—
is missed when the suffering of deep feeling is slowly removed
by psychology, safely installing the soul within the confines
of collective conformity. The wild poetry of Bruce Fessenden
escapes such a mundane and trivial view of life.

The poetics implicit in the writing of Bruce Fessenden can
be seen as a process of *memory purification*. The matters of
emotional memory are addressed, again and again, each time
with subtle nuances of difference. Memory as alchemical
refinement: purification as distilling confusion into the very
essence of emotion now spiritually valued, a way of giving
oneself—the greatest and deepest of all desires. Emotional
memory becomes "uncoupled" from the self. The words of
"self" may still carry the verse, but self gradually becomes
one with the subtle substance of the world, its sustenance,
its nurturance, making an open future, one that is not pre-
determined already by the illusion of "owning" our memories.

The poems are a progressive hollowing out, occurring in layers,
which lead to a dawning hope, but an almost unknown form of
hope, for we are forever confusing "wish" with hope. Emotional
memories, tended, tenderly so, open into silent space. Silent
space reveals the possibility of being possessed by the infinite
mystery of love, emotion now blending with the breath of
imagination. Hope does not desire anything for itself, as these
poems do not open to any longing outside themselves. Hope is
never "I hope that . . . " The unraveling of memory that occurs
throughout the poetry gives way to a new and indefinable sense
of relatedness, intimacy, and ultimate assurance, the assurance

of hesitation rather than the falsity of security that comes with unconscious repetition of the past.

The poetry of Bruce Fessenden leads us into intuitive awareness, fully conscious, a new vision—vast, bottomless, and incomprehensible—an invitation to a future toward which hope reaches and love gives.

Robert Sardello
Author of *Silence, The Mystery of Wholeness*

FATHER

Threadbare Coat

My Dad stands outside on the sidewalk
on his way back from the hobo camp.
Time magazine, coupon for toothpaste, whiskey bottle
all randomly piled in his walker basket.

Thomas map book open to a Berkeley neighborhood—
    he always likes to be clear about where he's going.
He's talking with the neighbors—he loves to talk.
    When I come down the stairs
    he asks for money.
I got a twenty in my hand; I beat him to the punch.
He talks with everyone
but he never takes the time
    to talk to me.

I'm quite a bit different than he.
    I never say a word to anybody.
I like maps. I curl up with National Geographic.
    I dream of far-off places.
I spend my days listening to the songs of the angels.
When I get restless I play with my toys.
I don't bother anyone, I keep to myself
    I don't make even the tiniest waves.

In the end it's the stillness that hurts the most;
in the end the longing tears me apart.
Hard asphalt
    weeds growing in the cracks:
    If you don't know where you came from
    you can't know where you're going.
Please come see me sometime and teach me some words—
    bring some food and a little water.
My hair is brittle and my lips are parched.
We were both the eldest.
    We share the same threadbare coat.

The world is made from darkness and light
twisting like the DNA molecule.
I drink myself stupid most every night.
    I'm that forgotten boy who never found his place.
    My throat is dry.
Dark springs gurgle in the cavities of my body.
I should drink more of that clear, cool water.

II.

There's an equal measure of chaos and order
    woven into the fabric of the world.
Once I had some talent and a few coins for giving;
    now the screen door is flapping on its hinges.
The cold cherry skies stretch from horizon to horizon.
    I'm licking the salt—
I think it might be doing some good.
A tree will never grow straight
    from a seed planted in rocky soil.
    Freedom for me is a freedom from hope.

They're penned up in back and they're brainwashed good
    they fetch a high price on the auction block.
I'm too receptive, yet I help when I can.
I still think there's someone out there
    who cares.
I'm blind and I'm broken, but I'll carry a little more.
    I'll leave a big tip—
    I don't want you to go out of your way.
Wrap me tight and brand the barcode—
    whistle's blowing; jammed tight and jostled.
    Our eyes widen as the train pulls away.

III.

He who holds the heart of humanity
    within His one heart—
    He is passing out from the pain.

She anoints His feet with oil
   and He is whole again
   momentarily,
the silence within the suffering
   like the leavening of bread.
What is the gesture being made
   through the humiliation, the despair of Christ?
What is being placed in the world?

Within my blindness and folly,
my relentless self-destruction
   inside that darkness
   lies a living grace.
Sometimes I feel it:
   a quiet presence
   hidden, young, mostly mute.
The foot soldiers of this world are fodder.
The discards, the worthless ones—
   they sacrifice themselves at every breath.
The abandoned and the forgotten,
   the blackened and the buried,
   they are often
   the ones who care the most.

I'm on the road; I burnt my maps for warmth.
The old neighborhoods I'm leaving far behind.
They bombed Mom's house;
   Dad was soaked in electroshock
   until he signed the papers confessing his many sins.
I'm wearing my threadbare coat; I've got my back to the world.
I'm running for that high nameless mountain.
I knew a girl once but I've forgotten her name.
   She gave me a piece of rose quartz
   before leaving me behind.
She slipped out the back door in the middle of the night
   her path as hidden as mine.

There was an Easter ceremony decades ago
   back when I was still a boy,
   when I was still wearing shoes.

The pastor held the service outside:
the sweet air, puffy clouds of early springtime.
When I think of the greenery, the billowing white air,
    I fall to my knees.
    My salt and tears becoming the clay of the world.

Quarters and dimes I give to the rich man up the street
desperation and openness I give to the world.

The Fool

I came from nowhere.
You took me in; you lifted your skirt—
　　you made me feel right at home.
We collected
marbles, old lamps, picture frames.
We scoured the second-hand stores
　　combed through basements,
　　the disorder of my life more perfect
than a movie star's face.
I slipped the old nun a few silver coins.
　　She handed me a biscuit made of corn.
　　She never looked up
but I could feel her praises.

The retarded boy is measuring his sticks.
　　Time is short—
　　he better get it right.
Too far to the left
　　and you're up against the rocks.
Too far to the right
　　and the current's unpredictable.
All that weight just slows you down.
　　I kept my troubles,
　　the rest tossed overboard.

My Dad moved out west, looking for a better life,
　　hoping he'd finally get it right.
Looking for order and harvesting chaos,
　　he imposed his will upon the world
　　in his own inimitable way.
We buried him in his crimson coat
worn at the sleeves and missing a few buttons.
The cops knew it was him by the color.
We held a remembrance at the boarding house—
　　we circled around the piano
　　and sang a medley of his favorite songs.

Camaraderie and good cheer flowed into the wee hours;
lady behind the desk was dancing a jig.
He and that lady
    did crossword puzzles together
    and complained about the wars.
Her time's gonna hang a little heavier
now that he is gone.

Tears of the angels
    plop out of the pine trees,
        sit silent on the forest floor.
I could have done better, I could have tried harder—
    I got no idea what held me back.
I sharpened my pencils,
    raised my hand in class.
        In the end the words never came out right.

But then most of us are just fodder anyway,
    just ballast for the passage of the world.
I patched my boat— I hope it floats
    on that final day.
        It probably won't matter much anyway.
There's more than one commerce
    undertaken in the back rooms of this world.
        Strange languages are spoken every moment of every day.
Your body's an instrument and mine is too.
    Let's hold hands and gaze into each other's eyes;
        we'll eat the biscuits and drink the wine.

I felt nothing for so many years.
    In the end I felt every feeling there ever was.
I am the rocks and I am the sky,
    my fumbled words and hesitant movement
        is where I'm touched by the world.
So small and so forgotten,
    I was here forever.
    I am that black grandmother baking rhubarb pie
        in a smoky cast iron cook stove.

Sit down and rest your feet; you're not going anywhere
      you'll never get
      what you don't already own.

I remember my father at the piano
      crooning so hard he's shaking the stars.
      He's wearing his crimson coat.
Angel looks at the beautiful world
      through our eyes.
      I'm here to help in any way I can.
I am the sun and I am the wind.
      I'll peel your carrots—
      there's no need to keep score.

Studebaker Hawk

I'm the oldest brother; I'm tilling my corn.
    I try to stay close to the ancestors' ways.
Mom buried Dad's bones near the remains of my brother.
Someone dug up their graves, took the turquoise and silver—
    probably sold it for a few bucks
    to the pawn broker in town.

Many of the native born
    fail to reach middle age.
Many die young and most die poor
    with the world moving so fast, so random,
    so helter-skelter—
    it's harder to find themselves a place.
But the angel can't see those
    who don't show their face.
What is the quality of prosperity anyway?
    Not something that can be bought or owned.

The runaway boy sings his victory songs.
    They use him because they know he'll follow orders.
The infantry charges and the walls crack open;
    prairie wolves feast on the corpses.
I need a little credit, I'm filling out the forms.
    Banker keeps asking me questions I can't answer.
A kindly nun taught me writing in school.
    I try to fill in the blanks—
    don't know why I feel so tired.

Wealthy businessman has taken a young bride:
    She was prom queen just a few years ago.
All of his fantasies soon to be realized,
    he's got no idea why he feels worse than before.
Never much for religion, now he feels like praying
    but the absence of words rings most loudly.
There must be a fall before there's any redemption
    but how do you keep from falling too far?

He lies in his bed, but he can't sleep—
    passage of time a wasting disease,
    a corruption at the bottom of his bones.

I'm native born—
    thick black hair, sun reddened skin.
    I'll always be an older brother.
Back door unlatched and I wandered out,
    a piece of carrion without much protection.
I was running from my past but I couldn't run fast enough;
    I carried my father's wound in my hot blood.
I built a bomb but I lost the timer,
    clutching my helmet and running hard
    trying to escape the fireball blast.

There's a blindfolded woman wandering in circles
    over at the refugee camp.
She's got flies on her lips and cobwebs on her head.
    They're asking for her ID;
    she can't remember her name.
The light's gone out at the bottom of the world—
    the angel is fumbling for the switch.
She can't remember what she came here for.
    She's facing north when she should be facing south
    as the world convulses in pain.

Down at the hobo camp
    the funny old man has breathed his last breath.
He loved to tell stories and sing bawdy songs.
    Often they declared
    that he was a natural entertainer.
Friend and foe alike, they toasted his life
    drinking rum and brandy from the battered pewter mug.
Scrap lumber and brush they gathered
    as twilight dimmed the sky.
They dressed him in his crimson coat,
    placed daisies over his eyes and mouth,
    a garland of asters for his head.

He was laid in the center of the combustibles
   a mandala poised for an offering.
Brandy and rum they poured over his body;
   a few urinated on his face and chest.
One of them tossed a glowing cigarette
   igniting the funeral pyre.
White skin blackened, then shriveled,
   soon just a gleaming skull.
They rolled and tumbled all night long
   singing his favorite songs with lusty gusto;
   then, much later,
   tenderly singing goodbye lullabies.

Next day they picked through ash and embers.
   Brass buttons from his crimson coat
   they found on the edge of the fire pit.
His charred bones they buried
   in the roots of a massive cypress;
   they divided up his meager possessions.
He had such nice handwriting, one of the women noted
   holding his journal
   though few of them knew how to write.

II.

Out in the prairie of eastern Montana
   a native woman lives in an Airstream trailer.
She's well respected in the community:
she gives wise council; when she speaks she's fully present.
She helps with children abandoned by their parents.
   Weeds in the garden might grow into flowers
   if you tend to them right.

Her trailer was listing to the south—
   over decades it slipped off its foundation.
When it rained, water ran down the walls
   puddled in the hall and soaked her carpets.
She built a planter box to catch the rain
   fixed it on the side exposed to the weather.

10

Herbs and vegetables, buttercups and daisies
    an offering to her kin who had fallen.
Her planter box garden: lime, red and orange
tiny splotches of color in the sunbaked prairie.

There's a timing to human lives:
    trapdoor is shut and the past gone forever,
    present moment a terror of isolation.
The native boy washed cars for minimum wage;
    his girl friend dreamed of something more.
He began working at night for a dealer.
  He sold dope and collected the money;
    he was naturally skilled at stalking his prey.
But the loss was already there, a taint in his blood;
    the innocent most easily sacrificed,
    movement of fate heavy and sure.

Perhaps he was distracted
    thinking about the future,
    not just struggling to survive.
The screech of police sirens, a high voltage shock,
    a moment of quiet and then the panic.
He felt his heart beating in his chest. Then he bolted.
    He slammed the car door on the officer's knee,
    he could hear the bones breaking.
It was over for sure but he ran anyway
    and the shots rang out in the night.
He collapsed like a puppet when the strings are cut.
    The officers kept on shooting and shooting,
    filling the corpse with smoke and lead.
Ungiven gifts, undeveloped love, unnoticed details
    that lived in his blood:
    an offering silently soaking the ground.

She was just an old Indian woman.
    Been so long since anyone
    had called out her name.
Another herb for her planter box,
    but lately she hasn't been eating.

When she was young she liked the fresh morning light—
   now she sits alone under the twilight stars.

She smokes a cigarette while feeding the chickens.
   She never smoked before;
   neighbors whisper that she's taking her losses hard.
There's a wrecked Studebaker up at the burial site
   scavenged for parts, vintage '62.
   She can see it from her kitchen window.
She's up there most afternoons.
   If it's cold or rainy, she sits in the car
   smoking her cigarette, an erratic breeze blowing
   through her dark and grieving rooms.

Famine, civil war, suicide bombings—
   hardship in every corner of the world.
Woman in the refugee camp selling fortunes;
   animals come to her and lick her hand.
Stick an assault rifle under their arm—
   the children are in need of an education.
World spinning out of control like a lopsided top—
   better step a little quicker or you'll get plowed under.
What is grief anyway but a wound of the blood?
   A rip, a gash, an opening into the unknowable.

She sat in that wrecked old Studebaker,
   stared at the sky, watched the seasons change.
Time an obstacle now.
   All of her kin dead and returned to the earth.
She kicked at the ground and thought her thoughts
   a tiny silhouette up on the hill
   backlit by the lavender twilight sky.

The days were crisp and the nights were cold
   when the idea came to her—
   an escape, a way out.

She carried kernels of corn in her pockets.
   When up at the burial site, she tossed
   the kernels to the wind and onto the dirt—
   she liked to look at the patterns.
Back the next morning to mark the changes:
   changes in the light, changes in the dirt, changes in the silence.

It was after a day of rain, ground still muddy.
   From her kitchen she saw a couple of teenage boys
   siphoning gas out of the Studebaker.
They were looking for trouble, looking to bend the law,
   looking for a way into town.
The tumblers clicked inside her mind—
   her body relaxed instantly.
   She stepped out of her trailer and smiled at the sun.
She had a pack of Marlboro's
   on her kitchen table.
   She lit one up; her first friend in such a long time.

What sort of feedback loop is grief?
   At any point it could go either way.
A lifetime spent in the weaving of the fabric—
   in an instant it gets torn away.
Nothing left but the memories now,
   memories of loved ones already gone.
Never was a place for me in this world.
   Why waste another minute of precious time?

She's sitting in the Studebaker, enjoying her cigarette,
   gas cap nearby, lying on the ground.
She feels no regrets, no fear, no anxiety,
   for soon all the suffering will end.
She inhales the smoke gently, her hand rests on the door handle.
Open the door, toss the cigarette into the tank
   sit quietly in the car
   and wait—
   that's the idea in her head.

One last look at the twilight prairie.
She feels a deep and abiding peace.

But beauty of the world is a messenger,
   a bridge to something more.
And suffering is a grounding—
   a link to who we really are.
She suddenly feels tired, feels it is time to go home.
She opens the car door, screws the gas cap
   back in place,
     tosses her cigarette into the burial site
     and with her toe rubs the glowing ember out.

III.

Down at the hobo camp, I built a marker to my Dad
   alongside the fire pit:
Couple of cypress branches still green
   lashed together with leather cord.
Bits of tile glued onto cardboard was the backing;
   I called it my harvest-day cross.
Last time I saw him alive, he raged at me,
   clubbed me with his cane.
Filled with self-hatred, yet generous towards others,
   I think he had a soul
but he lacked the vertical dimension.

Dad lived his life with drunks and thieves—
   the only support he ever knew.
Someone stole that primitive cross,
   his threadbare fate still beating strong—
   even with him in his grave.
Bits of tile wouldn't fetch a dollar
   at the nearby second-hand store.
Perhaps in an odd way
   he was a monk; the jewels of his life
   remaining forever hidden.

On full moon nights for the remainder of that summer,
   we built bonfires in the fire pit,
   held hands and sang songs until dawn.
His friends and his enemies, and many who never knew him—
   a celebration that can't be stolen.
He had charisma; he awakened the humanity
inside those who knew him.
   I wished he was there
   so he could see it.
Earth light is hidden, then sparks alive through communion,
   wicks up through dirt and grasses,
   up outstretched arms and to the sky.
I am the darkness and I am that clear steady flame.
   I will always be a son.
Shine a light and sing your praises
   for my Dad much more than me.

IV.

After his death I wrote a letter to my Mom.
   I'd had no contact with her for twenty years—
   didn't know if she was still alive.
His passing like a heart connection;
   I was numb for so long.
   Suddenly I missed her so much.
Just a week went by, package arrived in the mail:
   a ziplock bag filled with kernels of corn
   and the hood ornament from Dad's Studebaker Hawk.
   It was in her letter that I heard about my brother.

I remember a time when I was still a boy
   even then the Studebaker was barely running.
It was January and Dad was in the car—
   he went there often to do his drinking.
The sky turned black and it started to snow,
   wind picked up and it turned bitter cold.
I put on my gloves and woolen hat,
   found him passed out in the back seat.

I dragged him and carried him as best I could.
    Mom and I lifted him onto the sofa near the wood stove.
He woke up hours later and began to sing softly.
    He looked at me and
    for that moment anyway,
    there was gratitude in his eyes.

I dug up his bones from under the cypress tree.
    Placed them in the very same box with his brass buttons and journal,
    sent them back to my mother.
A late fall day, she's bundled against the cold
    shovel and cigarette in hand.
    Mercy touches the heart in the completion.

Heartland

Perhaps our next prophet will be a woman—
She's on the prowl for a little more pleasure.
She's bending over;
   I'm looking hard;
   I turn away when she looks my way.
She's trying to soften me up—
   she likes to look at my face
   when my feelings are blown apart.
She likes to see my light,
   see the stars through my body.

Or perhaps our next prophet will be a grandmother—
A peasant woman from the old country.
Her cheeks are ruddy;
she wears an apron everywhere she goes.
Her socks are bunched around her ankles
   as she enters church on Sunday morning.
She can smell the brandy on the priest's breath.
   She gives him a warm smile,
   squeezes his hand.

It might be the donkey
belonging to the dirt farmer down the road.
The farmer doesn't say much—works all day, everyday.
The donkey's all he's got.
Once the donkey wandered into the barn,
   ate a winter's worth of sweet potatoes.
Farmer works hard but the donkey works harder.
   Potatoes were grimy;
   the donkey never noticed.

Perhaps it's the field out back: everyday dirt,
   a well-worn coin, date rubbed off. A coin
   doing the hard work of circulation.
   the sacred more of a process than a feeling.

Pa tried to grow squash in that field
but the land was too elevated—in spring and summer
    too much direct sun.
Just a piece of prairie now: baby buttercups shining in springtime.
Eyes of a child will wick up that joy,
    for the world is filled with longing
    like an invisible tide.

There's a piece of me in everyone;
a piece of everyone in me.
I grew up poor and I grew up open.
I am made from earth below and sky above.
I am the springtime grasses
green with hope.
My blood is the rain, my eyes the stars,
my words the murmurings of the earth.
Mom was an orphan, Daddy a sharecropper
    he taught me to plow my furrows straight.

Old woman lives a few miles up the road—
up on the reservation.
She doesn't say much, but when she does
she sure gets your attention.
Face lined and leathery; turquoise jewelry and comb of bone,
    when her gaze lands on you it's like
    she's reading the stories folded into the petals of your heart.
Lives in a trailer with her cats and her dogs,
clips coupons, occasional cigarette, watches TV some.
I visited her when Pa was sick.
She gave me a turquoise ring. I kept it hidden in my coin pocket.
She didn't say much, just handed it to me
    when I got up to leave.
I don't think she did that too often.
    I don't think she gave much away.

You can feel it when you're at the center
    because there's only one center.
Feel the bite of a late fall morning—
    poplars lining the creek are a radiant gold.

Pa made me a toy wagon from scrap he collected.
   I can't remember where he found the wheels.
Come springtime, we filled the wagon with seeds.
he dragged the wagon out to the fields,
my hand curled up in his.
We're all seeds anyway—
most of the seeds scattered by the wind
but some of them take root.

Sometimes I think the land is in prayer.
Dirt farmer working the land as best he can
   and the land repays with the poverty of beauty.
Hands are dirty but the fingers are slim,
   silence of the land an invisible chalice.

Perhaps dreams need a period of dormancy
   like topsoil requires a fallow period.
Perhaps dreams need a melding with heartbreak and loss—
   a time of darkness and compression in the depths of the earth
   so new life can emerge.
Pa died too young; his name quickly forgotten
   but I remember the details of his life.
He harvested what he could,
   his gestures a quiet praising.

He got sick during the first drought,
   heartland turned to dust,
   hot winds stripped the topsoil away.
First a cough, then a trembling fever.
   He was released from his burdens pretty quick.
I didn't get along with Mom's new man.
I was still a child when I left for good.
The air warm, moon full
   that night I tiptoed out the door and headed south.

I found work on a trawler.
   They never asked for my papers.
   I spent my free time in the French Quarter.

She stood in a doorway dressed in red;
she caught my eye as I passed by.
We went to a bar, had some drinks.
    I found I could talk to her as she talked to me.
We went upstairs, but I don't remember a thing.
    I woke up next morning in the corner of a room.
She was gone, but she left me some apples
    and a bird carved from wood
    painted blue, underbelly painted white.

I joined a traveling circus—
    cleaned cages, fed the animals.
I wanted to be a tightrope walker
    but others could see I was suited for clowning.
The circus performed along the Gulf Coast in winter;
    come summer we headed north.

My heart is made from stuff simple and plain,
    just the dirt and golden grasses of the prairie.
    Beauty of the world a wounding
    I don't think I'll ever recover from.
Sometimes you have to go back to the past
    before you can step into the future.
    You move to heal your parents' wounds
    so you can begin to live with your own.

One night I slipped away; it was as if
    the horse knew where to take me.
I went to the reservation first—
    her trailer still at the top of the hill.
One of her dogs came to me,
    licked my hand.
Her door unlocked, but she was gone—
    returned to the earth, returned to the sky.

I headed down the road familiar
panic leaking into my body
    when the poplars along the creek came into view.

Just a two-room shack with a sod roof sagging
    filled with tumbleweeds, broken soda bottles and grit.
I felt the heat of the sun touching my skin
    the air didn't move—
    there was too much silence.
I found the donkey's bridle in the barn
    but I couldn't find what I was looking for.
A few yellow Kodachromes littered about:
    pictures of people I didn't know,
    a couple of Mom which I kept.

I spent the night in the old sleeping room
restless the whole time; I left at first light.
I rode north into Montana
    through fields of blue grass
    extending out to the horizon in every direction.
I rode for days through the heat of summer.
Cresting a rise, I came to the Missouri river.

I spent the summer in a hobo camp
on the banks of the river, with men on the loose—
    men looking for some sort of life.
Early one morning, I was checking the fish traps
    pinks and yellows of dawn
    wicking through my senses,
    reconfiguring my inner world.
I noticed it suddenly; half buried in the muck and brush
    of the shoreline, like a nugget of gold
    mixed in with the ordinary.
A flexi-flyer sled; I wondered
    why I hadn't noticed it before.
Probably belonged to a boy living on a homestead farm upstream.
    Perhaps a springtime flood had washed his farm away.
I cleaned the sled as best I could
    with river water; used a sock to rub it dry.
One of the slats had been repaired—
    piece of 1 x 2, looked like barnwood, cut and fitted,
    fixed to the rails with a couple of square-headed nails.

That boy was poor,
    yet somebody cared for him
    and I thought of Pa,
  the plug at the bottom of my heart loosened
    and grief welled up.
    Seemed like it was never gonna stop.
For me the cloth of life is woven
    from the threads of caring.
    In the end, life gets washed away
    yet the caring remains.
Pa had nothing; not even the dirt that he farmed.
    He was nothing in this world,
    yet his heart still here somehow,
    knitted into the mercy that supports this land.

I spent the day fashioning a primitive crib
    in the space between the rails of the flexi-flyer.
    I used twigs and bits of worn shirts
    that the men had discarded.
    I weighted the sled so it could float upside down.
When shadows lengthened into twilight,
I placed the turquoise ring and the blue-colored bird
    in the crib between the rails; floated the sled on the river,
    watched as it drifted to the horizon
then disappear forever.

I spent all night curled up on the bank of the river.
    I didn't move a muscle,
    devoured by my dreams.
Morning came and I rode south
memory of a woman etched in my mind
like gold script bordered by rubies.
I looked high and low, but I couldn't find her.
But I found work
    in a hardware store.
I'm saving my money
    soon I will buy some land.

MOTHER

The Hard Stuff

They're serving the hard stuff down at the waterfront bar.
Best to drink it straight
with a little bit of ice.
Grab your coat, hitch up your ride.
If you get tipsy you can cut it
with a little salt, or a green sprig of fresh mint.
Is it a movement towards death, or the journey of life?
It all depends on what you believe in.

My best friend's a comedian—
penetrating insights often shocking,
his behavior tipping into the wild and uncomfortable.
But wisdom and folly are interchangeable;
two sides of the same mirror.
All the laughter has awakened the angel.
Let's give her a drink, invite her inside.
In the end we're all treading water anyway,
the tender and vulnerable parts of life are
    for giving. Try it—
    you'll feel better inside.

They're stuffing their faces down at the convenience store.
They never consume enough
    to satisfy their needs.
Electronic stimulation hardens the senses.
Anti-depressants, prescription pain pills—
do you really function better when your feelings are frozen?
Shame and unworthiness might be
a portal into your particular and sacred wholeness
but you can't take the first step
    if you can't feel the emptiness inside.

My Mom was a seamstress, she worked for the big man
at night she did people's laundry
for a few pennies more.
I shot squirrels in the forest for dinner

with my uncle's old pistol
I stole the bullets but I tried to re-use them.
You can't buy liquor with government food stamps.
Mom didn't have much use for whiskey;
her daily life was the hardest stuff of all.

I rebuilt engines and I laid foundations;
I helped her any way I could.
The mystery of grace best seen in the details.
I didn't say much and I stayed hidden.
A wing is broken and it's ripping my coat—
or is it the beating of my heart?
In the end it's easier to swim with the tides,
longing vulnerable and unadorned
wicking up my feet,
up blood, bones and limbs
as the stars harden, and brighten, and glow.

Best to sleep it off out back; it's dry in the barn—
the axis reforms in its own time.
Donkey's licking my face;
she's after the salt.
I feed her an apple
someone put it in my pocket
when I was wobbling unconscious.
She's nuzzling my face, nuzzling my armpit,
sunlight filtering through the cracks in the walls
after a night of all that hard stuff.

Sometimes I think
the earth is an organ
for holding spirit
like the organs of my body,
like the body of time I have lived,
for holding the ineffable.
Dirt of my life
hardens into darkness,
darkness hardens into jewels.
Sleep it off in back, and I give it to you—

no reason to keep digging except to give it to you.
Battered tin cup, bobbing and listing,
just a few drops
and you're intoxicated for life.

Trouble Letting Go

Mom was an only child; she dropped out of high school
when her father died.
She was fourteen—the Great Depression devouring lives.
   Her mother couldn't cope.
Mom left school, looked for work.

Children hold the freshness of life.
   Refugee girl sells her sandals
   to help feed her family—
   the future hidden and unknowable
   but often you can feel its brightness.
Time passes and the edges harden.
   Is the center softening
   or is the center opening?

I wish I had a photo of Mom.
   She was here such a short time,
   I'm afraid I'll forget her face.
I remember the sadness,
that red was her favorite color,
   all that salty water,
the way she twirled her hair.
She had no personal agenda; she lived
   for family and friends.
   the petals of her innocence filled us with joy.
She was blessed ground
   from which anything might grow.
She expected to be used, and that might have been OK
   had she been fed
   a few scraps of precious love.

There's a miner; he could be anywhere
   working with pick and shovel, far down
   in some forgotten mine shaft.

Beyond fatigue,
   beyond isolation,
   surrounded by inky blackness,
   light from his headlamp flickering and weak.
He lost his maps; forgot his plan.
   He can't remember how he got here;
   he'll never find his way back.
Shovel dull, pick broken,
he trips over the gold nuggets; hesitates for an instant, then
   continues on with his business.
Everything abandoned except for his longing,
   grief his only tool—
   he keeps digging his way back to God.

When I was a boy, Mom cared for
   ten cats, a St. Bernard dog, and a duck.
   The animal population in our household always a little fluid.
She had her coffee and morning cigarette
   in the kitchen; two cats in her lap.
   one on her shoulder, another curled up
   atop her head.
Hands of the angels reaching down through the animals,
   the petals of her senses soft and vulnerable,
   the connection already there.
   Still she doesn't notice.

I sleep too much now, but I've stopped dreaming.
   I've never felt more alone.
Wide awake at 3 AM; I lie in bed like a mummy
   enveloped by silence, like an oversized coat.
There's a possum rustling about in the kitchen—
   it gets in through a hole cut for the drainpipe.
   I can hear it eating the garbage.

The heart of humanity forever young and fresh—
   that exposure is sometimes frightening.

As a child I played in Mom's closet,
   burrowing under her shoes,
   dust motes floating in the musty air.
Boys like me
   are like leaves in the forest—
perhaps the silent ones
   are the marrow of the world.

The village of our past lies near the border.
   Although the architecture is from another era,
   the town square seems oddly familiar.
There's a river flowing nearby,
   corn growing tall in the verdant fields,
adobe church sitting atop a low hill.

An invisible woman sleeps in my bed—
   I can tell by the imprint in the sheet.
Smell of skin so subtle and faint,
   most of the time I think I'm imagining it.
I have no memory of her face
   or the clothes that she wears,
   only that she sleeps on her right side.
Not near the order and not near the chaos,
   wisdom lies closest to the emptiness inside.

Grandmothers congregate on the corner by the plaza.
Skin like leather, eyes filled with summer starlight.
Hard to tell where the face ends and land begins,
   where fingers end and bread begins.
Baby cries, one of them rises.
Mayor passes by, nodding respectfully.

Dad was an artist but also destructive—
   transformation turned inside out.
He was an architect; he
   built homes of wood; warm and intimate
   in satisfying balance with the land.

He was a man of excess, trying to birth something
but in the end he couldn't let go.
   He created a life where he couldn't be touched.

He wanted a drink after Mom's funeral.
   I took his hand;
we went to the corner bar.
People at the service looking at me funny
   in my dirty Levi's,
the only pants I owned.
Dad had a rum and then another;
he talked the whole time, trying to make connection.

Dad was a fallen man;
he fell about as far as a man can go.
But all of humanity is fallen anyway—
fallen into suffering, into greed, into love,
   fallen into embodiment.
   Entry into the spiritual world
   is through the birth canal.
This world isn't a place of safety
   not a place for staying asleep.
All of us carry a piece of the future.
   We hold an opening,
   a threshold for love into this world.
Angels can only be present
   through our eyes and ears.
That opening can be terrifying—
   a falling and a breaking,
   a falling back to God.

The village of the heart
has been here forever; the village of the heart is always being born.
A modest house in a familiar neighborhood,
   children feeding the animals as I pass by.
The grandmothers give me their timeless smiles;
I feel like they've been smiling at me forever.

They ask what took me so long.
    I don't know what to say;
    I'm feeling a little light headed.
They keep on with their knitting.
one of them offers me some food
    and I realize with a start that I'm famished.
I take a room; I stay a while
but I know I have to go back.
I still got a lot of work to do.

Communion

I wish I didn't carry such grief—
    it hangs on me like an old debt
    that's never repaid.
I got a big house filled with rooms
    but the doors stay closed.
      I spend my time in the space underneath the stairs.
Sparrows and starlings nest in the eaves of the roof
I hear their songs when I crack open the window.
A little blue bird flew in through the opening, broke its wing
    when it smacked against the wall.
      I took it to the vet but it couldn't be saved.
      Ever since I've kept my curtains drawn.
My sunglasses are on, I should venture outside
    but the darkness is so comforting
    so close
    so known.

Too much fire sears the bones;
too much ice freezes the heart.
Family and friends all left for America
but I stayed behind—
I was always afraid of heights.
I steam the tuxedos, polish the buttons.
    Pleasing words roll off my tongue.
I go to church on Sunday; I walk the alleyways,
    brush my teeth in the evening.
This town never brought much comfort—
I've lived here my whole life and I'm always respectful.
    These days, it's just a place to die in.

I was in love once, but the stink from my father's house
    was more than she could bear.
Masters and slaves are joined at the hip.
I play with my marbles and eat my fish sticks;
    father's knife I keep in my desk drawer.
I finger it at night, I keep it sharp and gleaming.

An older woman works her fields outside of town
I've noticed her for years, never bothered to learn her name.
Her fields lie in the crook of the river.
    Don't know if she leases
    or has some sort of ancestral claim.
Prime bottom land
    belonged to the duke's family before the revolution.
    Land's been cultivated since medieval times.
Crumble down castle on the bluff above the river,
    timber and tiles long since scavenged,
    songbirds nesting and blue blossoms growing
    amongst the handhewn stones.

After the war they made a dam
    to control the flooding.
But I thought the discord of the river might be a virtue
    like the floods that oftentimes ravage me.
Sweep away the muck and the junk—
    maybe then I can start my living.
Fresh layer of silt from which something might grow
    I'm intimate with my inner gloaming.

She works her fields every day but Sunday,
    Donkey drags a dinged-up plow,
    future cleaving the soil of the past.
Everyone in town has a story to tell about her
    but no one can quite picture her face.
She lives in a trailer with her cats and a duck,
    donkey has a shed in back.
She likes to cook stews, tend to her herb garden,
    knitting sweaters is her way of relaxing.
She doesn't keep lists and she doesn't have a schedule.
    Her crops sing their death songs; she can feel it in her body
    the sweat and joy of harvest day.

I wish I knew what healing was;
I wish I could weave that garment.
I've got a closet full of hand-me-downs.

If I need a new look,
there's always something in the discard bin.
    I went to a party once
dressed in my Goodwill clothes.
Nobody noticed, nobody said a word.
    Maybe they were all being polite.
But then the beauty of the world is a gesture—
    a pattern in the wheat,
        the patience of the stones.

All that silence in my familial house,
    nimbus of my ancestors
    I never claimed as my own.
When the world is lacking fathers,
    the sons devour the crumbs
    because they are always famished:
    stars are not sparkling in their blood.
And when the world is lacking mothers,
    the tenderness of life goes unnoticed
    hidden in the everyday details.
I got seeds for eyes and pomegranate loins.
    I stand in the sun like any other man.
And what lies inside the fierceness of kindness anyway?

I'm not sure a person really exists
    if they lack a self.
    That was what I was thinking when she made her call.
I packed warm clothes, extra socks and a poncho.
    I didn't think twice—
I followed her out the door.
I was looking for the piece that was already there.
An elderly monk accompanied us;
    his faith had evaporated, he was in the grip of despair.
He'd fallen for a young girl living in town.

The monk and I followed the old woman
    through town, then into the mountains.
Lost in our thoughts and open to the world,
    we were silent the entire day.

As twilight descended, we arrived at a barn
   dilapidated and weatherworn.
Dry inside, with hay in the back,
   bins filled with sweet potatoes and apples,
   a fire pit for cooking.

Lay the kindling carefully, teepee style works best.
   If the fuel is dry, the fire will surely grow.
We peeled the apples and baked the yams.
   Darkness heats as it compresses, ice eventually melting.
   How long it might take depends on the person.
Wild turkey, looking for scraps—
   I cut his neck with the knife I carried.
   We roasted it for dinner.
I felt bad, like I'd killed a friend.
The old woman laughed,
said the animals were honored to sacrifice themselves
   for our benefit.

Up in timberline country, the husk drops off
at the highland meadow, where we spent our summertime days.
Rock and ice, tussocks of green,
   gnarled pines submitting to the vastness of the sky.
And who is that child?
   My body is plastic now; my heart reconfigures
      and reconfigures again.
   I feel more alive, though I
   got no idea why.
There were moments that summer
   I felt the land was quietly worshipping,
   my life a tossed-off offering,
   two baby finches held
   in the woman's cupped hands.

Monk came alive that summer
      like we all did,
   the body of humankind
   a blossoming vine.
We climbed trees and we tended goats,

the monk's bald head gleaming in the sun.
At night, over a fire, in that barn with the caved-in walls,
    we'd swap stories. I told of my long dead mother.
    His father, a violent alcoholic.
We wondered how our lives would have been
    if our parents were happy and healthy,
but there is much in life you can only guess at.

The old woman moved in the background, rarely spoke—
    colors of the flower catch the eye
    but the wisdom stays hidden.
One day, the woman knitted me a sweater.
    I don't remember her packing the wool.
    I didn't notice the vegetable dyes or knitting needles.
My old coat, worn at the elbows and missing a few buttons—
    I left it in the barn.
Pebbles and flowers that I collected during the summer
    I left in the pockets of that old coat.

Days glided by, peaceful as the wind
nights grew cool, sun lowered in the sky.
One morning, without much discussion
we gathered our belongings, headed back to town.

One of the fiercest storms in memory struck,
    ship foundering on the rocks.
A watery grave for many on board
but unexpectedly, a few animals escaped the hold
    and swam to shore.
When the townspeople came looking for survivors,
a donkey, a few goats, and a calf
were wandering on the beach.

The animals were wild eyed and agitated—
    monk and I led them back into town.
We stopped at the woman's trailer,
    sang to them; walked them in circles.
    They quickly healed,
    for an animal easily finds its center.

I raised pigeons, the monk got married,
  the animals stayed near the old woman's trailer.
She needed a cow, her donkey was old—
  in the end it worked out best for everybody.
My fertile ground dried up, hardened into bedrock
  then the diamonds appeared.

I go to the barn, eat the blackberries
  growing through the broken wood.
    I still feel tired, I still got a lot to learn.

CHURCH OF THE ORDINARY

Everyday Dirt

I'm from the old school, I don't do social networking—
I manage my vulnerability in my private way.
Burlap sack out back filled with everyday dirt;
   summertime, smell of the burlap
   held by the afternoon air.
My rituals have hardened like yesterday's bread.
   I'm looking for a way to warm my back.
Harmony might be preferable to truth.
   I'm listening for the words to come
   of their own accord.

The animals aren't feeling so good;
the green mother doesn't support them
   like she once did.
They're not eating and prone to panic;
they've stopped following the ancient routines.
Redwood groves,
   remnants of the forest primeval
   still hold the silence of 10,000 cathedrals—
   a living presence, nurturing the mystery.
But the bears aren't hibernating, bees disoriented and listless.
   I light a candle for the abandoned child.

There's the stink of death coming from the king's chamber,
   functionaries pacing the halls.
I break down the door—
   I know I can be impulsive—
   but the guards won't let me speak.
Priests intoning in Latin
   while workers with spades and shovels
   are digging the grave.
And what is that crazy wisdom living in my blood?
   To fan the flames of life,
   you need an earthly connection.

The world is made from darkness and light
I've been dreaming in purple, the color of royalty
where everything is done for you.
Perhaps the kings are the neediest of all.
And I've been dreaming in red, the color of lust.
I remember they buried Dad in a cedar casket
rimmed in crushed crimson velvet.
His face was pale like wintertime roses,
   his lips purple.
Those last few days I was a good boy—
   I cooked his food and I poured his wine.
   The prince can claim the world;
   the servant does what's expected.

Sand dial keeps tipping and tipping,
   bits and pieces that make up my heart
   pouring through the constriction.
I remember my grandmother; she never said much.
I built my house on her foundation.
I'd stay up in her attic when things got bad.
   She made me pancakes and she tied my shoes.
A strong spirit counts for nothing
   without a form that can hold it—
   realm of neglect is where the nuns are found.

And what is wisdom anyway?
   More than a thought process,
   more than a chemical reaction in the brain,
wisdom is a gift from the world.
But when the world is out of balance,
   waters of love compress into anger,
   everybody's timing just a little bit off—
   a little harder to hear
      the resonating individual spirit.

If I could, I'd tell that dying king
   that our earth and everything in it
   is a sacred icon.

Every detail perfect, from the smallest to the largest.
Our earth so generous, so patient, so supportive.
If I could, I'd give him some of that everyday dirt,
    stars and planets curled up within his seed—
    a little water and something will surely grow.
Give a little back, in words and deeds.
    The tree is strong now—
    masters brew tea for the servants.
The answer is that there is no answer.
    The invisible wind is stirring.
    Be still and have a sip.

The Blue Church

There's a man from the east—
   he moves like midnight, like all your bad habits.
   He carries the early morning light.
He has the most unusual hands:
   almost black, even the palms.
There's hard truths and particularity in his prayers,
   the richest vein found
     in the darkest parts of his wholeness.

It rips the ground and tears the sky—
   the beast can't get its fill.
My joints are stiff and my blood is black,
   pain of the world courses through our veins.
It starts right here and it starts right now;
   I'm stopping what I'm doing and making an offering.
The knives are sharp and the walls are hard,
   the sacred often found near the scarring.

My garden's looking rough, so
   I tried deep breathing; I went to the therapist
but I never learned how to give of myself.
That man from the east—
I ask him for a suggestion.
he tells me not to think too hard;
   my body knows what to do.
I have a bucket of dung, I dig an irrigation channel.
   I leaven the soil, but something's not getting through.

There's a sickness going around:
The angels have red eyes and high fever.
   They're forgetting who they really are.
Dizzy and light headed,
hard to have a direction when the compass needle
   is bobbing erratic.
They look for new boyfriends
or eat gourmet chocolate,

a fitness regime for slimming the body—
    then maybe they'll be noticed.

I followed my mother's hard road
    out on the edge, where it's rough and strange.
    I couldn't find my way back.
Couldn't find my way back—
    I suppose that's one way to commit.
Commit to loss at every turn.
    Inside the desolation
    lives a presence.
Behind the breath and under the dirt,
    my church so close, so intimate, so hidden.
The quiet salvation always there—
    an altar plain and tender
    at the back of the heart.

They're growing roses down at the hobo camp;
    our world naturally tips towards the beautiful.
Faceless men with forgotten names
ripped up and plowed under by circumstance,
their hidden and unacknowledged grief
    an aeration of the soil.
Percolating down and bubbling up—
    shame, rage and panic might be part
    of the greater wholeness.
Heat from the future, flour from the past—
    under the fear and unnatural inflation,
    invisible bread is silently baking.
The angels aren't perfect; their garden needs weeding.
    The angels need to be fed, too.

I sold my telescopes and scientific instruments,
    dirt of my life making me small.
    I suppose I was looking for completion.
I met a girl once, she lived in a tool shed
    in a forgotten part of town.
We drank rainwater and fed each other blueberries.
    She stuttered her words but I liked her songs.

I sealed my fate when I bought her some shoes.
When summer came to an end, she slipped away.
I still can't say what I got from her
    or what she received from me—
    pieces of the puzzle come in unexpected ways.
Some spirits are strong, some spirits are broken;
tide rushes out and the tide pools emerge,
    wild roses floating on the water.

My garden is singing now; death songs
    of the plants and animals
nourish the moon and stars.
I built my church—
    I built it from nothing
    because its nothing anyway.
Mom was abandoned as a child, so she abandoned herself.
Dad's whiskey jar his faithful companion.
    I ran away as a boy, and I'm still running.
I keep running into myself.
And who is that lover, and who is that friend?
    Resources are running short,
    but the beauty of the ordinary never in scarce supply.

I built my church from the junk
    I should have thrown out years ago.
I built it right in the center of town;
    right where it will never be found.

Tenderness

Where did your tenderness begin?
When did you dissolve a little,
slide into darkness,
turn yourself inside out?
The openhearted ones—
their hearts might fill up with fear.
Better to be a little brainwashed;
better not to feel so much.
You're tense and you're taut—
you just don't feel right,
yet curled up inside your fear
is your precious receptivity.

They taunt me, they spit on me—
they can't accept that I'm different.
There's darkness in the middle
   I hide out on the edges.
   My fear looms higher than the Two Towers.
I took a number and I stood in line.
I read the self-help books, but it did me no good.
I forget where I came from.
I work a little cheaper than the other guy
I keep my mouth shut; I promise I won't complain.

Where does it begin?
It's supposed to go up—
   instead it went down.
Supposed to get ahead
   but I'm stuck in the mire.
The angles are bent;
   I've got the wrong instruments.
I read the book, but its doing no good.
   Maybe I held the book upside down.

I guess I sold it too cheap—
   in the end I gave myself away.

I push the basket, collect bottles and cardboard.
    my friends are these stuffed animals—
    they tell me their stories at night.
I enjoy my coffee,
    play dominos with the grandfathers at Walnut Square.
    Those on the margins have all the time in the world.

I remember your stories, Dad;
I replay them in my mind:
Whitewater rafting,
    sleeping outside on the summit of Mt. Whitney,
    some snippet the old Indian whispered in your ear
    at the hobo camp.

I keep the drawings you gave me
    tucked in my flannel shirt pocket.
My brother shrugs them off
    as lunatic scribblings,
    but I see them as your sacred gesturing
    so that, through your creative expression,
    your angel
    can experience herself.
You give me a questioning look, Dad—
    you have no idea what a mandala is.

I trim their hedges, water their lawns.
    I'm just background noise.
I wouldn't want to live
in one of these gated communities anyway.
Intercom screeches
    making me jump; my truck stalls out,
    then I can't start it.
Security guard gives me a funny look,
    but I got my papers—
    I got nothing to worry about.
Maybe he'll lend me five bucks.
    I'll hitch hike back to town,
    buy a can of gasoline.

We've sold our soul to the banks and oil companies.
    Debt in the trillions—
    we're all shouldering the burden.
Car bomb going off,
    faceless man's got a detonator.
    In the instant before the flash,
    I remember the peace on his face
    as he was sleeping.

Dad had his longings, up to his final day.
    In the end it was
    desire that tore him apart.
I got a pocket full of quarters
    but the dollars have all been spent;
    I lost my future
    but I kept his wildness.

I received the seed, but the weather's been extreme—
    water pouring down,
    people's gardens overgrown.
Time to strip the husk away—
    I know there's something precious to keep.
Time to go out to the desert.
I want total disconnection, infinite shame,
    infinite boredom, infinite futility.
I want
    the donkey to be my guide.
I want
    to be ruined, so I can see
my true gesture to the world.

The condemned man is up on the scaffolding,
    hood over head, noose around neck,
    seconds to live; he's been numb for so long—
now he feels everything.
There's a hidden language in his body
    glowing like an illuminated script:

assassinations and glorious sunrises,
    groans of the lovers,
    baby's first smile, grandfather's last breath.
In the final moments he hears a song.
He's in his village—
    morning sunshine on his back,
    his mother preparing him breakfast.

The sensitive ones soak up the confusion—
darkness in the world growing
    as fast as the light.
Heroes think they have the answers;
    realists just keep on sleeping.
Boys like me, we take on too much,
    carrying the pain seems part of the bargain.
    Our bodies are permeable in ways we don't understand.

The young novitiate is badly traumatized—
    he's listless; prefers to be alone.
The elders give him a room with a view to the east
    where morning colors
    of lavender, orange and red
    can move through his senses
    and seep into his soul.

He's instructed to light a candle four times a day—
    meditate on the beauty of the sunrises
    and the glittering midnight stars.
He's allowed two meals each day
    he sings and prays with the other monks
    in the congregation hall.
Otherwise he is silent the whole time,
    for then the larger silence of the desert becomes his silence
    as the joy within the singing
    awakens his heart.
A senior monk leads the boy back to his cell,
    The boy trusts him and begins to relax inside.

The old monk has learned
   that many who come here are broken
   and decades may pass
   before healing arrives.

Fruit will ripen on the vine
for that is the natural expression of the fruit.
Within the beauty of the desert
   there is a wisdom inexpressible.
Daytime light piercing and pure,
   midnight moonlight spun soft and close.
Wisdom of the land like folded hands
   best received through a tender and open heart.

I picked up your clothes, I filled your glass.
   I walk quietly through life.
   I leave the tiniest imprint.
I was still like the morning,
   elusive like the wind.
   Grief within the summertime sunshine,
   like bread and wine
   served at the Last Supper.
I fed your donkey while the stars hardened.
I think you noticed me,
though you never said anything.

OFFERINGS

Benediction

I was born into a world where
   words were a lie, where
   every word like a brick or a baseball bat
   are the words dead
   or are they an entryway into something larger?
I was kept in a closet and fed table scraps.
   My timing was off
   I held the key—
   I forgot how to use it.

There's a man on the overpass; he's yelling at the cars.
He's raw like an arctic aurora borealis,
like a four-dimensional being in a three-dimensional world.
There's a quiet humming in the in-between spaces
   of a soul cracked apart,
a quantum glow of rage and wildness
from a place beyond the stars.
He's making his offering, yelling out his piece of the puzzle;
few would flap their wings with such urgency—
few would sacrifice so much.

My last coin of beauty's been spent.
I'm down to white Penny's tee-shirts,
striped tube socks, three pack for five dollars.
All that longing bartered away,
predictable and ordinary all that's remaining.
I'll make my offerings anyway
from the ordinary part of my heart.
Wintertime stars shine in our summertime body,
corn ripens from springtime mud.
Rap music plays from a speeding Honda,
two homeless men talking big as they push their baskets—
all making their offerings, all nourishing God.

Bullies and victims live inside my body,
their disputes and battles turn my soul dark.

I was a king once, and I was a beggar—
I offered gold and rags came back.
It's an uneasy piece: the axis forms for an instant
    before the settlements are relocated.
Weapons are sharpened and martyrs walk the valleys—
    you can roam the world
but you'll never escape yourself.

Swirls in the sand, patterns in the wood,
cold weather clouds backlit by the moon.
Rub off the dirt and rub in the oil—
    each life a sacred icon, reconfiguring the earth.
Swirls in the sand, an offering hidden and silent.
    Tide recedes—different pattern comes back.

I was murdered more than once; the details seem to change.
They drained the swamp but they never found the boat.
I did what they told me and I couldn't make it stop.
I parroted their words, but was cast out anyway.
Deeper you go the more unhinged you get,
    but the more you have to offer.
I lived on the other side of madness.
I grew carrots; I enjoyed the silence.
The brain is a sieve but the heart is an oven:
the world comes in and bread is offered back.

Most resurrections go unnoticed now.
It's a helter-skelter world—cups are flying off the table.
In the beginning there was the Word.
    I've lost my voice, but I'm still feeling something
    my body yearning to make a sound.
I suppose
    the gold was always there; I wasn't small enough, or plain enough.
    I washed my face; I should have kept it dirty.

The shame is old anyway.
Most of it breaks apart.
    It hardens; you can hear the thumps
    hitting the ground.

Gold nuggets scattered about for the taking—
how odd that no one bothers to pick them up.
You can always give a little piece of your tenderness;
    it's never in short supply.

The fool sacrifices for the others; the fool is the first to fall.
Words that connect
    humans to the cosmos
    scattered about like Milky Way stars.
These words are gifts from the world
    and we are the instruments—
    the speaking requires no energy at all.
I learned to live
in that place of pure poverty.
I was nothing in the beginning,
    nothing in the end.
What I offered was never mine.
What I offered belonged to the world.

Trade Winds

I see you down at the docks
playing dice with the sailors.
Your eyes are turquoise; a silver parrot on your shoulder.
You approach, I panic. I lose my words.
My neck is tired; my skull like steel—
I'm spending too much time alone.
Not really here, but not there either.
My beat's a little slow, yet opportunity
    arrives in its own time.

I'm sipping a beer;
    you're knitting me a pair of socks—
catcalls from the sailors flying about like migratory birds.
Chill winds of autumn blowing through the cracks of the known
    backlit by the darkness of change.
My borderline is a bit indistinct,
    yet my shadow deep and sticky.
Your face a shock and a recognition—
    a break in the predictable,
a rift in my routine.

Saint Francis carries his innocence in a wicker basket
    he travels light—
innocence is all he needs.
A piece of the big bang living in everyone:
is the candlelight or the inky blackness more eternal?
You can't go looking for joy because you already have it—
    the world gave it to you first thing.
Storm is blowing, the animals run for shelter.
The well-to-do hunker down in their bunkers;
    the fool takes it square to the face.

II.

You live in the highland moors.
    Who would think that love touching and fiery
    lies hidden in that vast desolation.

I suppose I'm ready for anything—
    I have my knives and I have my salt,
    the nimbus of my body damp and yielding.
They say the skin is permeable to the other world.
    I've always had thin skin—
    that might not be such a bad thing.

Seven white horses galloping over the highland meadow;
    they trample the gorse and snap the laurel.
Are they in panic or are they an announcement?
Our world is ever steadfast, yet breaking every moment.
The sky's turning black, storm clouds roiling thick and deep.
I take off my brittle coat as the wind rips my face.
I bow my head to the ground,
    two baby finches nesting in my cupped hands.

How could anyone be as fierce and merciful as you?
You are unacknowledged, unnoticed, unnamed,
    yet close to everyone's suffering.
You must be broken, too.
Seven steps to your temple, seven moons in your crown,
anguish in my heart is my road back to you.
The world's topsy-turvy, yet they're still serving tea.
The final revolution will occur in the human heart.

III.

My toenails are split; my hair is thin.
I think I'll have a glass of wine.
Deeds run down and words run out—
    what's left is the silence and the mystery.
I buried my dead, but I kept their chairs at the dinner table.
Now I'm serving you and I'm biding my time.
Foolish wisdom is what I know.
I saw your face for a moment or two;
    sometimes I panic.
I am the flower—I blossom because of your love
    and I get frightened; I'm afraid that my luck won't hold.

Invisible trade winds blowing strong,
    sail of my body has turned inside out.
Saint Francis is with the birds and the animals, but I'm left hollow—
    that empty space is my piece of you.
You experience the world through my eyes and my ears,
    but you stay hidden—
you nurture the darkness.
    You live in the not-yet-formed.
Close to the ground and close to the suffering,
    near the dirt of the earth
is where the angels are to be found.
    Near the dirt of the dregs and the misfits
is where your footprints are to be found.

The trade winds are blowing, polishing the sun and silvering the stars.
Senses and skin vulnerable to your ephemeral touch,
water and mineral mixed together, yielding the rose.
I forgot most of what I learned, but I remember your face:
    lines of the unknowable often the most beautiful.
Seas heaving soft and warm, birds in the air—
    think I'll spot land before too long.

On the Border

When the epidemic hit our town
   the world cracked apart.
Bodies piled up and burned,
    ashes mixed with lime
    scattered over the fields, or buried in the forest.
Bells in the tower for someone every few minutes,
    then the ringing stops.
Silence the loudest of all
    passing through me like water
    that the rag of my body wicks up.
In the plaza, a wheelbarrow heaped with dirt
    sits alone—
    wooden handles, metal wheel with wooden spokes,
    shovel jammed into the dirt.
Solitary gull floats down, lands on the fresh earth.
    Looks right at me.

You can smell the stink, yet the flower seller keeps coming around.
In crazy times
    you do what you can do to keep life going.
    Perhaps that's the greatest service of all.
Then she is gone.
    I find her cart in a nearby alleyway.
    I place flowers on the doorsteps bordering the plaza.
Wind blowing like every other afternoon.
I feel the summertime sun on my back, like an old friend.
In the beginning, and in the ending
    there is only one truth.
    How odd, that when the trumpets blare and life is washed away
    I would feel such a glimmering.

I go down to the wharves.
I leave my bride on her dying bed; she has forgotten who I am.
    Without a home now, without a place or a name,
    who is the pilgrim serving?

Down at the docks
   a juggler performs with a clown—
   the clown in thick gray face paint,
   crazy crooked smile.
Small assembly watches them, throws coins at them.
Nobody bothers to collect the coins—
   not even the beggars.

The clipper ship is anchored in the harbor.
   I hear it sails through the Mediterranean
   north to Lisbon, then across the seas to the New World.
I'm seeking employment; I find the captain in his office,
dirty red scarf wrapped around his face.
He runs the other way.
I go to the tavern across from the docks,
but the bar is empty, black mark on the door.
I pour myself some wine,
sit by the window, watch the shorebirds,
   watch my thoughts.
I leave a few coins on the counter,
turn the latch, walk out the door.

Who is listening anyway
   with my ears and my heart?
   Am I really still alive
   or am I a ghost?
If I keep speaking my words,
   perhaps the angels will keep singing their songs.
My life is a ritual now, stately and somber—
   my death even more so.
But I am still a human; I am here to help,
   the sacred best found in the caring.

I burn my bride's body down by the river; I take no precautions.
   I smear my face with her ashes.
I dig a pit and I lie in it; move the dirt over me.
   My face I keep exposed to the sky.
Afternoon sun beats down and I burn and sweat,
   then the day softens into twilight.

The sky turns marmalade, then pink.
    I sponge up the color.
    I can hear lambs bleating in the distance—
    it sounds like they are hungry.

Next morning I smear my face with more ashes.
    I go to the overlook
    where the wild roses grow.
I'm scattering her ashes amongst the roses
when a boy from town approaches.
He's a small boy, but with large hands.
    His eyes are wide, but he's not scared—
    he watches me in silence.
I remember his face, but I can't recall his name.
    In this world of death, a name seems almost arbitrary,
    yet connecting with a living person more precious
    than all of the blessings from all of the saints
    all rolled into one.

He's carrying a water bag made from animal hides.
    He offers me a sip.
Goatskin swells when soaked; when the weather's hot
    the bags hold water for weeks.
The boy must have filled the bags at the highland spring—
    water so cool and crisp
    you can almost taste the wisdom.

He follows me back to the plaza
where I gather the flowers I left on the doorsteps.
We walk together back to the river.
He helps me fill in the pit I dug the day before,
    then we plant the flowers in
    the fresh dirt.
The boy moves with a quiet dignity, but he never says a word.
When we finish, he vanishes over a rise.

You can't see the dark matter, but you sure can feel it
    in your lungs and in your jaw,
    in the marrow of the bones.

Heavier than lead,
    it soaks up light like a sponge.
So heavy it collapses in on itself—
    darkness and fatigue implode into tenderness,
    hands of the world always hidden;
    two children swim back to the shore.

Donkey carries a blind monk across the plaza.
    I follow them into the church.
Doves cooing from nests high in the nave;
    dead bodies piled in the pews.
The smell isn't bad; someone sprinkled the bodies with lime.
For some
    the rigor mortis of death a beautiful mask.
    A few look like they might be friends.

Monk lights the candles, I speak the response.
We load bodies onto the donkey
    to be buried out by the sea.
The world dries out, hardens, turns brittle—
    a loud and inaudible cracking.
A baby cries out, the doves awaken
    billing and cooing rolls off the walls.

Days and weeks go by.
    The worst of the epidemic passes;
    the sun grows hot and the rains stop.
I carry water from the highland spring
    down the switchbacks to the monastery.
Five-foot pole across my shoulders, goatskin bag on either side—
I carry two per side if there is an urgent need.
Weight of the pole hard against my shoulder, weight of the sun
    harsh on my face,
    one step in front of the other,
    afternoon breeze drying the sweat.
Every moment I am receiving something—
    blood vessels are permeable
    and so is bone.

In their quiet way, the monks are welcoming.
    If I hadn't come here with my losses,

I couldn't have sensed the grounding.
Monks work the field while I collect beeswax
    or polish the ancient brass candleholders.
Twilight time, we assemble and sing our praises.
    I water my desolation and I walk the tightrope.
    In spite of all the sickness and death, I am no longer afraid.

The ground is fallow for a period
    so the wisdom of the earth can return to the soil.
Whittle a stick,
    cook your fish and vegetables over the coals,
    feel the warmth of the fire.
Under the stars, under the moonlight, a girl walks the beach.
She wears a red cloak, collects seashells in a basket.
    When the morning comes, she is gone,
    but her footprints remain.

Grapevines on the southwest side of the hill,
    peach trees in the afternoon shade.
Have a slice of peach—
    net of the body harvests the light within the fruit.
Summertime sun shining strong and sweet, on-shore breezes,
    wild roses blooming up at the overlook.
Feel the warmth on your face—
    there will always be more than you will ever know

It's Christmas time now, and I am feverish.
I've carried the sickness for a long time.
The monks are gathering around my bed,
    their quiet presence a great comfort.
I'm afraid that I'm contagious.
    when I express my concerns, the monks just laugh.
My time has come—a song is welling up from within my body.
    It seems like we are all singing.
The song stops, then starts
then stops
then starts.
Turn on the light:
there are others in this room I haven't met before.

HEART IS A VORTEX

My Soul in Love

I never had time for homework; I cleaned stables,
    played baseball. I was exhausted, even as a boy.
I was respectful yet distant, I sacrificed my cruelty.
    I always aimed to please.
Piece of me huge and dark went unclaimed and forgotten.
Songs of the addicts cut the deepest—
    all that tenderness spilled to the ground.

But in maturity
    most of the tree is dead anyway.
Life force concentrated in the roots and the crown.
Sometimes I wonder if death is sacrificed for life
    or is it the other way around?
Pain can be like a family heirloom, passed from fathers to sons,
the ravening beast never gets his fill.
I walked in circles but I never got started;
    I carried the yoke of his destruction.

You knew I was damaged when we first got together.
If you want to give me anything to remember you by,
    just give me a pistol.
I tip toward isolation like I tip toward beauty—
    now the madness has grown full flower.
You lived in a single room when we first met:
    harsh whitewashed walls, a little too bright.
I gave you my roots; I weeded your garden.
My blood turned grey and I became invisible.
I live like a monk but I'm generous and supportive;
you lived by yourself and you felt you were nothing.
Innocent as robin's eggs and wild like the wind,
our vines grew together for a while, but how can I commit
    when I can't commit to myself?

Time is my enemy now, cold and hard.
I always believed love would find a way
    and I suppose it did, but for somebody else.

I've got my compulsions and my mismatched clothes.
  I stand naked and I stand aroused, but the wind has shifted
my ship blown onto the reef.
  I sang pretty for you and I was plowed under,
my ugliness fertilizing the infinite ground.

Two angels in the upstairs room—
  they're yelling and arguing; neither one holding to a plan.
I wish I had a son or a daughter to love.
I tried to love the world, but it wasn't enough.
  Trumpets blare—
the petals of my particularity are blown apart.
Over time, the delicate flower silently reforms.

Your brother is crazy and I'm crazy, too—
couple of lonely crosses at the top of the hill.
You talk about growth like it's a well-mapped geography
but the razor wire of your fate is cutting your feet.
Perhaps you should serve your suffering tea and tasty biscuits:
  you can't get any sleep—
  starving child crying in the night.
All that research,
  so little is known—
  statistics and numbers, computer projections—
everything is captured
  except the life.

The fool gives and gives until he breaks apart,
  fumbles for the quarters in his pocket, and gives a little more.
There is no map for the wilderness of love.
  Crippled old woman lives on my back porch—
  she won't sell her body for a million bucks.
  Desperation and surrender she gives away for free.
That broken old woman is shockingly beautiful.
  When I least expect it,
I can catch her singing my name.

You tell me, my love,
    you want to escape the trauma, flee the pain,
    but your wounding like a trail of breadcrumbs
    leading into the darkened forest.
Those breadcrumbs are for you and you alone.
I can tell by your face that you don't eat enough.

Blowdown

Storm's coming up, gonna blow big and long;
gonna blow all the walls and corners away.
Blowdown filling the street, wind out of the north—
icy dark wind straight from the Bering Sea.
Events swirling about like autumn dried leaves,
    tipping point tumbling along the pavement.
Organs and senses harden into husks,
    compress,
then implode into light.

Pressure dropping fast; gauges are exploding,
sandpaper wind blowing paint off the walls.
My blood is blue and my organs are orange,
skin and hair unraveling out to the horizon.
Grief trapped in the eyes, the fingertips, the throat—
banshee winds stripped all else away.
Angels hum their laments, but the ground isn't listening:
electronic chatter has rendered the world self-absorbed.

My third grade teacher, Mrs. Crittenden
showed me a picture once:
wild animals clustered about a watering hole.
Rain pounding on the roof of the school,
she fed us graham crackers and we took our nap.
Storms raging inside me then—
    still raging now—
drops so big and heavy they'll crack my skull.
Always had my guard up—running for cover,
    running from my past, terrified of my future.
Hanged man lives at the top of the hill:
    thick security walls, heavy iron gate.
    If you go up there, you better bring your I.D.
Up on the hill, in the fury of the storm,
panic in his blood, his eyes bulging and vacant.

He carries his noose and he carries his scaffolding—
    everything else left behind,
but his love and his fate he can't live without.

Quicksilver girl at the refugee well
    drawing buckets of water for the masters.
They broke her feet so she couldn't escape,
horns of the animals ground into a powder—
rich men often pay for a little more performance.
Brown skin and strong blue eyes,
my tipping point might be close at hand.

She looks at me and I'm feeling the heat of the spotlight.
Nimbus of my body glowing a little brighter
    when she draws near;
only desperation and prayer nourishing that young heart.
But you can't become whole without first being broken—
wise ones say we all share the same heart.
Love was always there, hidden and unrecognized.
That worthless detail, that dirty and buried place
    might be where we find ourselves.

After the storm hit there was only darkness—
nothing left but my grief
    illuminating the path.
I grew up poor and I grew up unnoticed:
everyday dirt gives birth to the rose.
There are places in me where the ground has laid fallow—
    fear and doubt an unexpected composting.
Who can name the future that might emerge from that silent soil?

Quicksilver girl; with me for only an instant,
feeding me food that I'll never name.
She takes my hand but she can't run.
    Now I'm living for her—
petals of the flower form around the suffering.
What is life anyway? Her captors would never understand.
It all gets blown down, yet something remains.

Aurora Borealis

Many in this world live close to darkness;
   many live in a cloud of unknowing.
Perhaps there is darkness
   to better feel the touch of the light.
   Perhaps there is darkness
   as an entryway into the heart.
I came here with nothing—
   no place, no name, just a body.
I came here with all I need;
   in the end my practice is one of recognition.

As a young child, I hid in the background.
   I didn't say much—I was already touched.
I spent my afternoons
   staring at the fog
or transfixed by the soft shape of Mt. Tamalpais
   filling the sky to the north.
I was five years old; I had some friends,
   but my best friend
was the silence of the land.

Dad was a minotaur; he trapped me with his rage.
   Mom's interior sun eclipsed by her grief.
I was six when I first ran away.
   I was like Mom—abandoned by the world.
   I climbed a live oak and curled up in the branches.
It had thick bark like elephant skin,
   grey-blue feathered birds flitted and tweeted in the crown.
Afternoon sunshine warmed my skin and hair,
   evening stars filled my eyes.
I read somewhere
   that Milky Way stars were hundreds of light-years away.
I didn't know what a light-year was,
   but when I looked at them,
   I felt like I was part of something larger—
   that the holes in my heart

morphed into roots
binding me to the invisible ground.

Drunken man wobbled down the gravel road below,
    singing his brains out;
    singing to the bloody stars.
Old country lane leading to nowhere—
    he has his jug, so he doesn't care.
Just grist for the mill, like the children and the nuns:
    he's serving his time
    worshipping life in his own way.

I always had problems with relationships—
I failed the evaluations the experts gave me.
I couldn't feel much; I sat at the back of the classroom.
They said I looked a little stunned.
Am I overwhelmed, or is some part of God
    emerging through me?
Do I isolate because of the terror
    or to remain in touch
    with the rawness outside?

I lived my life in trailer parks—
    I didn't do much with my time in this world.
I cared for my cats and cared for my birds.
    At night I drank my food stamp wine.
I rebuilt carburetors for a few bucks.
    Whenever I could I slipped away
    to the High Sierra mountains.
Granite and light,
    lakes scattered like blue jewels—
    I came alive in the high mountain air.

II.

I read about him in National Geographic
    in an article on Inuit culture.
He was a healer; he restored
    the spirit of those who sought him out.

One woman said it was like
    being touched by the aurora borealis.

He could have been any of us—
    a drunk or a nun,
    or lonely boy living in his mother's closet.
He lived in an Inuit village in the far north,
    his little town located aside an inlet,
    a low ridge providing a bit of protection
    from the shrieking gales.
He was too quiet—
    wouldn't play with the other children, or do his schoolwork.
    Months passed, and he never uttered a single word.
Teachers and social workers noticed, of course,
    but none could get through.
So many broken souls in the native communities of the north
    with resources drying up, it was assumed
    the boy would end up as another statistic.

But a tribal elder saw something different:
    the misfit perhaps the bearer
    of the greatest gift.
He taught the boy his native language,
    the ancient stories and songs.
The two of them spent months at a time
    in the woods, walking the forgotten paths.
The boy learned quickly,
    As he entered his teenage years, it became unclear
    which was the student,
    which was the guide.

The boy grew into manhood and was a healer—
    many said he was the best they'd ever known.
His greatest virtue
    was his patience and capacity for recognition.
    He felt it in his body
    when he found the piece he was looking for.
Once he had a man collect honey from a bees nest.

Another time,
    he had a woman travel hundreds of miles
    to sing a song to her father.
He never gave explanations.
Sometimes the treatment came quickly.
    More often, he spent days looking,
    usually without food or sleep.

He never took money for his services.
    One woman paid with loganberry jam.
He only worked with those he knew.
    He could have been famous—
    instead he kept himself small.
He had no personal relationships.
    When not working, he collected shells at the beach,
    tended to a colony of feral cats.

He built himself a home of whalebones on an elevated piece of land
    above the trailers and out of the mud.
He caulked the walls with pitch,
    lined them with bearskins for protection from the winter's cold.
The roof was sod and the floor milled alder,
    cedar and larch burning all day and night
    in his two wood-burning stoves.

The messenger moves from town to town, because
    he has no place to call his own.
Elusive and quick, he slips through the cracks
    and into the church, or the neighborhood tavern
    carrying nothing but his grief.
Not of this world or the other one, either—
    inhabiting some in-between space.
    Bringer of light—
    the heaviest burden of them all.

He was in his mid-twenties, and life seemed tranquil,
    the village more prosperous than it had been in some time.
Then, in late winter, a series of storms struck,
    each more ferocious than the one preceding it.

Raging winds kept everyone inside—
   to venture out was courting death.
Ten days passed before the storms abated.
   Snow was chest high in the streets.

The sounds of his cats alerted the villagers.
They knocked on his door, shouted out his name,
   but they could feel the emptiness already.
His door swung open and there were only the cats—
   no sign, no note, no nothing.
He disappeared into the teeth of the storm, leaving no tracks—
   just a few seashells and food for the animals
   and a photo of a woman no one knew.

Women of the village
   maintained his whalebone house.
On the anniversary of his disappearance,
   everyone lit candles
   and circled around his home.
The nights were still and frosty; flame burning peaceful and steady
   like his spirit, and like yours too.
Often the aurora borealis was crackling and blazing overhead.
   Why do those lights touch the heart,
   some wondered.
   Why is the unknowable so moving?

                         III.

Dad sold me cheap
   to pay off an old debt.
   I left his house; I've been walking ever since.
My mirror is cracked—
   I look misshapen to myself,
   but I can see into two worlds simultaneous.
The healing gesture towards the world
   is one of submission.
   What is longing anyway
   but a desire to see God's face?

                         78

In the final moment, the Inuit healer
   removed his clothes and ventured into the bitter night,
   hand in hand with his personal silence.

And where does the mystery of wholeness touch you?
Where is that wound, that shame, that poverty, that hidden temple?
The ineffable stammers and stutters in all of us;
   the blind man hordes his jewels by giving them away.
Time is short now; the veil is thinning.
   Once the seed is planted,
   it might be better to let go.

Silver and Gold

Could be anyone:
doctor or lawyer, beggarman, that man over there in the silver Benz—
probably works in commercial real estate.
Could be anyone:
stranger, child, mayor—
when you walk through the door
   you walk alone.

It's a tourist town; the old church looks out of place—
   made in the olden ways: adobe, stucco, rough-hewn pine.
Massive door, iron hinges heated and hammered:
   craftsman's long dead, but what he wrought lives on.
Lilies with elongated stems intertwined
   etched into the hinges, carved in the wood.
In former times, the particularity of a person
   was considered a gift.
Door creaks when opened, yet it's well balanced—
   swings easily in spite of the weight.
Air inside is cool and musty. When you breathe,
   your body relaxes.
I have no idea why.

Patterns in the wood, enhanced with stains.
   Your pattern is a little more hidden.
You're the queen of our second-hand store:
you reign over the patchwork quilts, the musty old books,
   used Barbie dolls with broken limbs and glass eyes.
You stopped eating years ago and I worry so.
   Hard to get your nourishment
   when you're living only on light.
Regal yet funny, your cup's always filled.
   You never plan ahead; you have another glass of wine.
   You have faith the land will provide.

You plowed the earth, hammered the silver;
you said you weren't much of a craftsman—
you did better than you think.

You composed our garden with your suffering.
　　Such a small plot.
I suppose a well-balanced door can swing both ways.
You sold your pearls to save your kingdom—
you already reserved your little white room
in the other world, over on the other side.

Old church sandwiched between mini mall and apartment building—
　　the sacred often found nested within the ordinary.
Light turns green, tourists rush by.
　　For many the church doesn't exist.
Wooden cross, cracked and dry,
bleached by the sun, held up by rusty wires
now slack and sagging from the passage of time.
　　Yet the cross remains silently standing.

I thought I was depressed, but I was expanded.
　　I curled up on your porch,
　　hair clumped and matted.
I lost my homeland, my voice melted away.
　　It was as if you were talking to my guardian angel.
　　Is it because you'd already sacrificed yourself?
We talked about the weather, made silly little jokes—
the quilt of intimacy woven from minor details.
People like you safeguard the love—
　　yours is the generosity of a fool.

It's always the final day with you—
the final hour, the final gesture.
Won't you please eat some food?
You need your nourishment; the world isn't ending just yet.
You are radiance and you are golden—
I suppose some must step aside
　　before others can step up.
I'll clean your room if you put down your wine.
　　No more purging—
you've purged enough.

They march through the old world village,
boots clomping on cobblestones,
    brass band playing slightly off key.
Marching through the fields, around the cemetery,
up the goat path and onto the ridge, beneath the afternoon sky.
Singing the whole time, they pause at the top
and begin to toss blossoms red and pink:
    dozens, hundreds, tens of thousands.
Driven by the wind, held by the silence,
the blossoms float out to the horizon
    and wink out.
Music plays on, twilight sky hardens into darkness
    like your past hardens inside your body.
We stay hidden, you and I, hidden like a couple of fugitives.
Yet the face of mercy is everywhere
    more hidden than us.

Better pack your socks, bring some eggs and cheese—
perhaps a craft of a good Italian wine.
You don't take anything, you trust the world,
    the grace you've accumulated
you've tossed back to your friends.
I'll give you my quarters—I wish I had more.
Yours is the hardest path I've ever known.

I tried to pay for my life with my darkness—
    the most beautiful thing I own.
I'm that solitary figure working long hours in the forest.
    My chain is dull; saw making a racket—
    I never heard the humming of the angels.
You gave me your scarves
    and Alta-Tadema prints.
I held them for years
    but I never gave them away.

It's a hot afternoon, band playing in the plaza
    beneath the massive church door.
Trumpets and tubas, drums and accordion,
    the fiddle player looks battered
    looks like he could use a drink.

Brassy and melancholy, a little crooked,
    notes reverberate off the whitewashed walls.
Children stop their playing and grandmothers nod
    as the procession slides by.
Weddings and funerals, they look the same—
    a link with something unknowable.

Wolves prowl the high pasture, they stalk the lambs.
    Think I'll take some of the red blossoms,
    rub them into my sore.
Or build a fire, grind up some seeds,
    make a tea, drink it before bed.
They say love is everything, and I believe those words are true,
    but love is a slippery fish
    that keeps sliding through my nets.
I am haunted and you are strange.
    I'd like to think
    our common denominator is sacred mystery,
    but I fear its something darker.

There's a time for beginnings and a time for endings,
like the moment I had my first breakdown.
Dad's violence leaking into my body,
    my world reconfigured forever.
Or when you had your first drink
or first heard Mahler—
    fireworks filled your sky,
    your body filled with song.
It's one step forward and two steps back—
who can say which is the preferred way?
If I wasn't so raw, my senses wouldn't wick up the starlight;
    songs of the whales sounding over lavender waters
    wouldn't seep through the cracks in my head.

You better pack some instruments: a compass or a map,
    a sextant for reading the stars.
You think you need nothing; you might be right—
I know you're at ease in the invisible land.

But your boat is so small,
   still waters black and cold—
   human senses are warped in that eerie half-light.
Just a crown of flowers and some tossed off regrets.
   Your footprints are fading,
   but the light in your heart shows you the way.

My fear is a piece of the mosaic,
   a turn in the labyrinth,
   the bruise on the apple.
What did I bring you, anyway—
   you who are more hidden than I?
You walked through this land,
   your wicker basket filled with red flowers,
   wolves licking your hand.

I broke my back because I fell too far.
I never should have set foot in this world.
I am the misshapen cavity
I am the resonant pit nobody ever noticed
I am the lumpy stranger singing the song
   nobody ever forgets.
The world is careless now, yet the fruit has ripened,
   ready for the taking.
I'd rather be desperate than asleep—
   ugliness gently pulled down by currents in the heart,
   prayers for the ineffable come out the other side.

Everything you did, everything you could have been—
parents and grandparents, obstacles, triumphs—
   all that was just loaned to you.
Loaned to you by the world;
   now it's time to give it back.
I paid you in silver—I wish I paid you in gold.
   What's done is done.
all that remains is the Nocturne, the Slow Masurka.
You're slipping away, but your dances live on—
   your dances belong to God.

Confusion reigns:
red blossoms dropping from the palms
    of the angels outspread hands,
They're copying you,
    but they can't match your ease
    or your grace.
    They thought you were one of them.
The angels look up to you—
    follow you around.
They can only experience life
    through your sacred particularity.
    You keep forgetting the door swings both ways.

The Candle

Most of my friends have sunk into depression—
   a sea of black mixed with islands of light.
They tell me they gotta fight dirty
   in a corrupted world, those that cut corners
   are the ones that get ahead.
They can't feel anything, except that they're missing a piece,
   suffering like the wick of a candle.
   Humans fall into darkness
   to better see the light.

I'm driving my car, the traffic's bad.
   I plow ahead, but I'm not getting anywhere.
Ball game on the radio, I struggle to pay attention.
   Don't recognize the players;
   don't know who to root for.
August 1st, where did the summer go?
   Bite of autumn in the evening air.
Am I a pilgrim or am I a refugee?
I wake up in the morning feeling strange.
   I should have brought a map—
   I'm wandering around in an in-between space.

Sometimes I think all the gadgets
   are in the way of life.
Useful as a convenient distraction
   for avoiding the truth of ourselves.
Sometimes I think the angel is confused
   because of the electronic chatter,
   harvested organs, bioengineered seeds—
   she can't feel
   the direction of the living.

Lazy Sunday mornings, we used to snuggle under the comforter.
Easy to find connection then.
I liked to lick you,
   watch your nether parts ripen and swell.

A tangle of legs, the smell of salty fluids,
    the compression of the world temporarily forgotten.
But the vortex of life that brings people together
    also tears people apart.
Forty years I spent with you.
    I'll always love you; don't know what I did wrong
    don't know why it didn't work out.

But then longing is like an invisible tulip fire—
    all that breaking and all that shame
    collapsing, then reconfiguring;
    darkness shimmering even more than the light.
I packed your bags; I'll drive you to the train station.
    Please call tonight; I need to hear your voice.
There's a presence tucked away
    inside the grief and aloneness, deep in the heart.
    If you haven't heard her lament,
    you haven't sacrificed enough.

II.

A homeless man is living in his van:
    I heard his story when volunteering at the soup kitchen.
He's a Vietnam vet, couple of years older than me.
    He looks for work when county funds dry up,
    but the hiring people can see
    that he's lost his spark.
    His van's over by the park.
    The cops know of his past; he's not violent—
    they just let him be.
Lately he's been complaining that he doesn't sleep well.
    Says it's the pills the doctors give him.
    When he wakes up, he can't remember where he is.
    He should feel hungry,
    but he's lost his appetite.

Often at night, because he's awake,
    when the moon is bright he slips out of his van
    and hikes up into the East Bay hills.

He follows fire roads and deer paths;
  if he's lucky he can find a good flow.
  His body feels more alive in the darkness.
He looks for clearings in the pines and the brush
  or an overlook with a view to the west.
He likes the silence of the pre-dawn hours,
  hardness of night softening into early morning light.

He has cornbread in his pocket—
  a woman at the soup kitchen gives it to him.
  She's concerned about how thin his face looks.
Breaking the bread into chunks,
  he tosses the pieces into the wind—
  an offering to the morning songbirds.
They dive in, a mélange of darting movement.
  When the crumbs are gone, they vanish just as quick.

Months go by, his nocturnal ramblings mirror the cycles of the moon.
Then early one morning, a Scottish terrier
  emerges from the bushes,
  fur matted and tangled. That dog has been long abandoned,
  is terrified and starving, as the man can plainly see.
He breaks off a piece of bread,
  places it on a log, then steps back.
The little terrier approaches, vulnerable as a baby's first hour.
Suddenly she gulps down the bread, though
  the morsel not normal canine fare.

He returns often to the very same clearing,
  brings kibble and treats for the dog,
  a bowl of water left behind.
Time passes; the dog begins to trust him—
  licking the man's hand, curling up in his lap.
One summer morning, he carries her out of the hills,
  down the trails and fire roads
  in the crook of his elbow, back to his van.

He volunteers Thursdays and Sundays
   at the soup kitchen: washing dishes,
   helping with the clean-up,
   terrier befriending everyone.
His name is Charles; he's still living in his van,
   but he's got a direction; he looks happy.
   He looks like he's got enough for now.

III.

As for me, I'm living alone now,
   feeling old and ordinary,
   still gripped by my compulsions—
   part of me is dying so some other part can stay alive.
I wake up tired, although I'm not doing anything
   except wrestling with my angel
   all night long.
It's not even my body anymore, not even my heart.
   Sometimes the emptiness becomes a presence—
   her love burning, such a clear steady flame.

Acknowledgements

I'm a quiet person. I don't say much; I find it difficult to ask questions. Yet so many stepped forward and offered their help, often just when I needed it the most. I have never thought of myself as a writer—I began writing to better understand myself and my world. My heart must have been open, as support came my way, and I am so grateful.

Thanks to Beverly Charles, my first writing teacher.

A big key for me was the courses in writing I took from Andy Couturier. He calls his series of classes "The Opening," and really, that what happened to me—I opened up to myself, my soul, my truth, my experience. I went past the barriers and into the substance.

One of the many skills Andy has as a teacher of writing is the capacity to give incisive feedback in a way that nourishes both the writer and the writing. All of his students were supportive of my efforts, especially when I was mired in self-doubt. In particular, Tobie Shapiro, Johnnye Gibson, Jody Savage, Barbara McBane, and Katrin Arefy helped shape these poems.

My editor, Jane Brunette, has the gift of seeing what was trying to be born, inside my images and words. Often it was a nudge from her that opened the door.

My partner in life, Chris Bergren Fessenden, a lifelong artist, was an ever-present sounding board. I could tell if I was headed in the right direction by reading to Chris. She gets it immediately.

Robert and Cheryl, you opened my heart. Your guidance and wisdom echoes through every one of these poems.

Thank you Jerry and Jo Tennant, for the use of your cabin at Tahoe City, where many of these poems were written. A cozy cabin in a pine forest near the lake—I love that cabin and I love writing there.

Thank you, Rose Wong, for climbing with me in the High Sierras. You encouraged me to challenge myself and push against myself. The climbs we did together were both a digging down and a purification. Interesting that the capacity to believe in oneself is given by others, outside oneself.

Finally, Mary Jane Taylor, your book cover design is incredible! There will be some who will buy the book just for the artwork.

About the Author

Bruce Fessenden has been a climber and skier his entire life. He is best known for making the first American (and second overall) ski descent of Denali, the highest peak in North America, in 1977. He has also done ski descents in Mexico, South America, and throughout the mountains of the American west. Deserts, forests, beaches, and especially the high mountains have always been a sanctuary for Bruce. He is still an active climber and skier, as well as a mountain biker.

Bruce's interest in soul life began when he was in his early 20s, in parallel with his ongoing struggles with depression. He began writing in the late 90s, in response to the Columbine school shootings. His involvement with the School of Spiritual Psychology started in 2002. Bruce feels that the beauty of the natural world is a kind of scripture that the body reads at every instant. He feels that human woundedness is more of an invitation to enter into something deeper, than a problem to be overcome.

Bruce is co-owner of Fessenden Firewood, a business he shares with Christina, his friend and partner since childhood. He lives in Berkeley, California.